Racecar Jesus

Racecar Jesus

TRAVIS MOSSOTTI

POETRY

THE **BLACK SPRING**
PRESS GROUP

First published in 2023
by The Black Spring Press Group
Eyewear Publishing imprint
Maida Vale, London W9,
United Kingdom

Cover design by Josh Mossotti
Typeset by Edwin Smet

978-1-915406-55-2

*The editor has generally followed American spelling and punctuation
at the author's request.*

BLACKSPRINGPRESSGROUP.COM

In Memory of David Clewell

TRAVIS MOSSOTTI's
previous collections are *About the Dead*, *Field Study*, and *Narcissus Americana*. His fifth collection, *Apocryphal Genesis*, won the Alma Book Award and is forthcoming with Saturnalia Books. Mossotti has been the recipient of the Miller Williams Poetry Prize, the May Swenson Poetry Award, and the Christopher Smart-Joan Alice Poetry Prize, and he currently serves as a Biodiversity Fellow for the Living Earth Collaborative at Washington University. He lives and works in St. Louis.

TABLE OF CONTENTS

Who are these coming to the sacrifice?

—John Keats, 'Ode on a Grecian Urn'

BLACK HORSE, WHITE HORSE, BOTH PLASTIC

– after Vallejo

I will die as predictably as the elders I've watched
(and continue to watch) dwindle—
even fireflies have a season, and then what?

I watched the fireflies, too, after my funeral
where I floated there dumbly: the coffin
like a fishmonger holding out a mackerel to a buyer.

My wife and children have watched me sleep
like that, only, with less gravity. My mother,
of course, the milk sour on her breast,
must have stroked my hair in the darkness.

My daughter is in the yard outside the window
while I'm writing this poem—potatoes
cooking in the oven. She has two horses.
She's wearing galoshes even though there's no rain.

      Not even a threat.

For, behold, the Firebird Cometh

...we are each of us born so holy and everlastingly
molested.

—*Adrian Blevins,* 'November Neurosis'

BREAKFAST WITH MY SPIRITUAL ADVISOR AT SUNNY SIDE CAFÉ

His first job out of school was working
as a hospital chaplain at Mercy,
sat bedside with the dying

for a living, and he tells me what
it was like to wait for the joints
in their fingers to go loose like he

was letting the fish steal the hook to swim
back off into scripture with.
Out down the road

the early service releases and a ringing
tower sends off the congregation
with the old, irregular style bell

ringing that signifies to me an actual
human is somewhere down there tugging
one end of some rope that crashes

a lead tongue against the hollow insides
of cast iron. You hear that, I say,
pointing with a slice of bacon to the air,

and he says they're an expression of joy
meant to help us forget our sadness
for a minute or so, and I say,

it's there though, pointing at my heart
with the bacon, the sadness, even
when we let ourselves forget it,

same as it's always been,
the heartache and the thousand
natural shocks that flesh is heir to.

He says he prefers Blake
over Shakespeare any day of the week
when it comes to either sadness or joy.

To see a world in a grain of sand, he says,
and a heaven in a wild flower.
When the ringing quits

I say, I prefer Frank Stanford, which
is a damn lie, but I don't tell him I actually
prefer my wife's hair slinking down her back,

though I do, or that I prefer sneaking out at night
for a cigar on the porch in early fall,
or that I'll always prefer to bury the light

and put on the darkness like a pair of wool socks
with a hole in one of the big toes
over Milton or Jesus or Sappho.

There are houses so broken
they aren't worth fixing, and sometimes
that's exactly how I feel. Waterlog turned

to dryrot turned so useless you couldn't
sink a nail. Sometimes my wife whispers
she loves me from the other room and all

I hear are bells. Other times, there's only
a lonely wind passing through the storm door
whispering almost nothing at all.

HOTEL

From my top floor room I see the Washington
Monument bathed in pre-thuderstorm light.
It looks alone out there. It looks as lonely
as I feel standing in this window shirtless
giving not one thought to some voyeur's
telescopic lens touching me. I miss my wife
and children. I think it's okay to admit this now
to you in this space where we are both alone
and not alone in that weird poetic way. Hello.
Let me put a shirt on real quick and invite you
into my hotel room to stand on the throttled
carpet and talk about negotiating intellectual
property language for industry contracts.
It's just something I do from time to time.
Like how I might say a stroke of lightning
behind that phallic monument seems relative
to one's perspective, not meaning to make things
entirely uncomfortable, but you know
the phallus as well as I do makes people shift
in their seats. Maybe we're all just vessels
of orange light glowing the way coals do
in a fireplace towards the end of a night, but
hotel rooms don't have fireplaces. My house does.
I must rely upon my belief in the existence
of worlds beyond this one, lives beyond this life
I'm still sorting through, time that expands
beyond the need for time to a universe where
clocks are set to night-blooming cactuses
or the twirls of octopuses. I think you desire
as much from existence as I do. Do you
think of it as a sponge you're wringing dry?

Maybe that's just me. Maybe I'm the storm,
and maybe you're the monument rising
like a microphone from an empty stage.
I think if I try real hard I can actually see you.
Go ahead, say something. Say anything
that makes me believe you're actually there.

ECCLESIASTES

This girl at my daughter's school said her family
lives in a mansion, and now my daughter says so, too,
as we cut through the rich side of town and
drive past homes with tennis courts and heated
stony grottos that waterfall into mosaic tiled pools—
inspired by the ones in Santorini no doubt—and statues
of angels that rise from the center of the pools and blast
trumpets, water tumbling down like a musical note
only the wealthy can hear. Her family must be blessed,
I say, even though I know the girl lives in Shrewsbury
where there are no mansions to speak of, only bad debt
and potholes and troubled parishes and racism, and yet,
our house, which is not in Shrewsbury, must seem
tinier each day to my daughter. She's not old enough yet
to be embarrassed by the claw foot tub and moldy vanity
and giant hunk of underlayment and linoleum I ripped
out from the bathroom, set on the porch, because of mold,
smelled it like another emergency loan from the credit
union. Thank God we had a deep enough porch to store
the junk while we figured out how to finance the job,
me providing the labor and it's a wonder I'm still not
drinking. I'm saying that the bathroom has decorated
our front porch since February and it's spring now,
and Cora's getting older by the minute and must see
porches that aren't warped and leaning and weeping
the contents of the house. Listen, I'm trying to tell you
that I'm writing this poem and contemplating a tub
in front of me that's turned on its side like one of those
sad whales washed up on a beach with fifty pounds
of plastic in their bellies. I'm trying to say that I wear
a sports jacket to work because I've worn through

the elbows on my shirts—people at work think I'm
putting on airs, but I'm actually just cheap and desperate
for something in my life not to wear out. The jacket
was my father's and each time I slide it on I feel him,
but how the fuck did we end up talking about me? Let's
get back to the mansion my house is not and the daughter
growing taller and wiser by the second and the truck
I'll need to borrow to get that tub off my porch
and the bathroom in disrepair while the crocuses
have come and gone and now the daffodils and
soon enough the naked ladies and mulberries
and blackberries and when I was young there was
a moment when I thought money was the salve
one spreads on the wound of poverty and so my
friend and I drove up to a mansion we admired
in the middle of the day and knocked on the door
to ask the owner what they did for a living. Nobody
answered—middle of the day, the two of us skipping
school to get high and trespass. Maybe there's
a lesson I'm missing that's buried somewhere
in these words and I should probably just try
and remember how to pray or go read the Bible.
But a freight train is cutting through this two-sided
town and I can feel the porch vibrating underfoot
and the train's so loud I'd be foolish not to hear it.

ONE ART

By now, I've learned how to kill honeysuckle,
how to buy pants that fit today without shame,
how to transform a cellar into a rumpus room,
how to move quietly in the kitchen without
waking the house, although, I'm sure my wife
would have her own thoughts on that last one.
Ours is a small house, you see, a kind they don't
make much of anymore. Ours is a wild yard
we court for bees, butterflies and birds—
there seem to be connections all around us
that have taken half a life to fully appreciate,
synaptic tissue in the dirt that doesn't suffer
words like prodigy on principle. The best days
end with soil under our nails we can't quite clean.
The best days end with my wife's head resting
on me in bed and me stroking her long hair
in the dark. She asks if we're going to make it,
and I say we are, although, there's a great much
left to endure, and we've still got habits to break,
pain to compartmentalize into grief. The worst
days aren't much different. The worst days
are riddled with chigger bites and nostalgia.
The worst days remind us that the longer
we live the more there is for us to bury,
but that still means a shovel's involved and
earth and a bit of muscle to guide us—
a process we can lose ourselves in and recover.
I'm saying these things not because I want
to be right, but because I've seen the pink
of sunrise diminish into fuller light more
than once and seen the same thing in reverse

at day's end. We're going to make it, I say,
in a dark house that listens as it sleeps. We're
going to make it. I say, We're going to make it.

SANTA CLAUS

When my daughter asked, I told her the truth, but part of that truth was a lie. I said, he doesn't exist, but when I was five, the red heft of his velvet ass flashed before my eyes as he squeezed up the chimney of my childhood home. Maybe it was a dream, she said, like when I heard what seemed to be his reindeer landing on the roof. Maybe, I said, both truths exist. As an artist, I said—but you're a poet, not an artist, she said—Yes, as a poet, I said, you must protect the un-seeable from those who project themselves and tell you what you see is all there is and nothing more. See what I mean, I said, her eyes drifting toward the window, a nearby rustling.

ANDY WARHOL CRASHES THE GRAND OPENING OF SCOOP-DEE-DOO, A STRIP MALL ICE CREAM SHOP IN ELLISVILLE, MISSOURI: 1986

I. Tangerine Dream

Part of me wishes I could go back
and warn the owners about overindulgence,
about that bright-eyed optimism that led
the entire Boomer generation

into underfunded retirements. Not that it
would've mattered. Nobody listens
to the future any more than they listen
to the past, and nobody in Scoop-Dee-Doo

but me could've even picked out Warhol
from his entourage, even though
it should've been obvious. Every circle
has a visible center, and this one

had a sweet tooth for Tangerine Dream.
I heard him between licks say, *This is lovely*,
flashing a gracious look at the owners
who never imagined a grand opening

quite like this: owners of the surname Stock:

husband: accountant by day, wearing
                     a pink apron embroidered
                     with a question: *What's the Scoop?*

and wife: former PTO vice president
                 and ex-high-school cheerleading captain
                 who'd never known failure;

both of them trying to smile away
the knowledge of a Baskin Robbins
slated to open up in the strip mall
caddy corner to this one,

and even the deliverance of Warhol,
master of soup-can wisdom, zeitgeist
of Americana culture, had no power
to save this place from itself.

II. Prelude

Three nights before the grand opening
we were invited to dinner at the Stocks.

They served my family homemade
funnel cakes for dessert with three extra

shakes of powdered sugar, and my dad
drove us groggily home saying,

You know, franchises start somewhere.

III. Blockbuster

Warhol in the 80s looked like
a three-week, cocaine-fueled bender,
so frail and diminutive,

sitting cross-legged
under the putrescent neon fritz
with a giant orange scoop dribbling

little streams of melt
down the neck of that giant
waffle cone and onto his hand.

This is lovely,

he said to nobody in particular,
as the world crunched in
on all sides, as Blockbuster,

which shared a wall
with Scoop-Dee-Doo, quietly
worked backchannels

with the strip mall owners
to knock down that wall
into the ice cream parlor

to expand their New Releases
section because even
a behemoth like Blockbuster

was feeling like the slow boat
in rough seas ready to capsize
under the weight of too much cargo.

V. Going and Gone

Two months? Three?
How long is a dream
even allowed to last?

Warhol died a couple
years later and the Stocks
are up there now too

handing Andy another
cone and massive scoop.
But for one brief instant,

every bit of improbability
held its tongue, letting us
believe in the permanence

of decadence, letting us
forget that one part of all
arrival is the whisper

of departure, that we
deliver our delicious ideas
to an expiring world

full of a knowledge born
too late and riddled
with ignorance.

SUPERIOR OAK RIDGE LANDFILL

Sagrada Familia, Gaudi's grand cathedral
in Barcelona, remains unfinished,
counting its way up to eighteen spires:
twelve apostles, four evangelists,
virgin mother, and Jesus. And people
in that city have grown up watching it
grow up for generations—the architect
dead and buried inside—the world
turned digital, cellular, the latest phone
snapping a picture of a spire, another
amateur who imagines he's got a grasp
on things, that he's worldly, that the world
is somehow fixed because he's captured
an image of it. Steve Jobs died a few years
back and will soon be obsolete, too.
His best inventions are now radioactively
leaking into the sea, incinerated into smoke,
or buried in the Superior Oak Ridge Landfill,
which I'm passing on the highway now—
landfill I watched grow up from humble
beginnings, smelled it hanging low
for thirty years in the valley, every
summer, every time I neared
the Meramec river. And when the county
council finally ordered the landfill to stop
accepting trash, said that it was
to be capped with clay and vegetation
and monitored for methane levels and leakage,
I felt a sense of pride for having watched it
grow up to the height of its brothers,
for having contributed my small part to it,

for knowing that one hundred years from now
this hill won't be bald, and this valley
will take back its slopes, and the river
will go on drifting its dumb course like a mule
that never grows old or tired or stubborn.
To build a building is one thing, I think,
but to build a feature of landscape
from garbage is another, and Jobs, Gaudi, Christ
have simply become names without owners.
What if I told you that when I was a kid
I followed the train tracks that brushed past
the base of the landfill, hiked up to the rim
looked over and saw an open pit alive
with the beating of a thousand wings,
the largest murder of crows I've ever witnessed
rifling in a field of trash that smelled
like nothing of this world. Imagine now,
like I did then, that any moment
the land could've risen into a conspiracy
of feathers. We think what we see is only
the half of it, that the capped landfill won't
outlive Gaudi's cathedral, although it will,
that the tallest spire isn't Jesus after all,
just our own ambition in lockstep
with a body we can't imagine is disappearing,
although it is, and so we build things up
higher than the one who came before
and we marvel at the advances until
the din of our creation sounds
like an electric insect rubbing its legs together,
and soon our summer nights are filled
with the hum of its mating call.

ART FAIR

I came to meander through open-air booths erected
in the name of self-taught metallurgical fiends
who curl lengths of iron into abstract lawn décor,

in the name of grade school art teachers
who scrawl feverish landscapes into the night,
in the name of potters who breathe and bellow fire

into backyard kilns, in the name of woodworkers
who turn burlwood into bowls for still-life prints.
I came here because there exist people with second lives

that last longer than the first, and because we all
eventually fall into the shapeless crowds who wander
these grassy lanes like ghosts who've fallen

into portraits tacked in museum galleries. If I fail
to bargain down a smear of moon oil on canvas, just watch
me move in on that bloodwood cutting board,

or that hand-twined chandelier, because there's a price
in my head that's incapable of change and all it takes
is a bit of small talk and to look someone in the eyes?

I once convinced a man at a roadside fireworks tent
to knock ten bucks off a 12-pack of Mississippi Gambler
mortar shells so I could paint the night with more color

than you can imagine, and he just sat back into his body
and his impossibly quiet lawn chair. Just sat back down
into a life defined by a carnival tent of powder and fuse.

Listen, I came here to feel a rougher art rush through
each one of my eye's billion vessels, because color
and form, and because far from the Louvres

of the world artists still find ways to fashion
grief into the arcades of other people's hearts.
Because somewhere near these tents meat smoke rises

from pork fat spit into embers, and because somewhere
there is a moveable stage upon which a bass player
slowly unlatches his case, and because soon enough

the lights of this art fair will begin to dim, and each
one of us will drift back to the silence of our homes
where we will each unearth from slumber the stud-finder,

level, hammer, and a single nail in order to hang
an image upon the dining room wall
where before there was nothing, until now.

FIREBIRD

Every man should sooner or later
custom build for a mid-life crisis
a backyard fire pit out of flagstone
and buy a '73 *Smokey and the Bandits*
Pontiac Firebird Trans Am T-top
painted white with a blue phoenix
power posing, wings spread wide
on the hood like glory be to sleeve-
less shirts and shoulder tattoos and
the boohoos for Tiger Woods and
his spine all but failing like a refurbished
carburetor replete with slip fit bushings,
his sad muscle rev of out of some bunker,
which is metaphor only for the sandy
foothills of the Mid-Atlantic Ridge
above which drifts the floating plastic
of future continents, and, *I'm too old*,
says the seagull to the dumpster
behind the Sunday sports bar wherein
every man sits watching Tiger charge
back to the leader board with pitcher
empty of all but hope of refill,
keys jangling in his pocket as he shakes
loose the last drops at the urinal
and zips in a hurry to hit the road
in his flame-wielding bird of prey
knowing Tiger will rise like the phoenix
regardless of his idle watching
so he might as well drive wildly home
and finish the night alone now
at the edge of his fire pit, might

as well stare into the tender coals
and hope the hopes of average men
flicker and pop in the fire going out.

YOUR RACIST UNCLES

More than one dead or dying uncle undoubtedly
springs to mind and perhaps a whole
lineage spitting archetypal arcs of Pabst

Blue Ribbon onto red coals at barbecues
for the pure enjoyment of fizzing steam. Uncles
who evolved from trilobites into middle-school

peeping Toms sneaking out Tuesday
nights to spy with borrowed binoculars
on Karen or Debbie or Martha, girls who

never looked back through the glass
to the dark outside that was your racist uncles.
A lonely, thickening syrup began coursing

through their aging heart's ventricles with fear
cruising fast as hummingbirds into flashes
of predictable outbursts at country

club dinners. Your uncles flitted like butterflies
in spring with their racism. Pillow slips
turned yellow under them as they slept.

Ceilings turned Marlboro brown in the scourge
of curtain drawn afternoons spent
peeking out, and hate became a cure-all Advil

your uncles popped from the medicine
chest into the blades of their mouths
to crunch and swallow on cloudy

days threatening rainbows. Your uncles
drove keen spikes of light into the yard
when night curled a tail around its nose

and slumbered. Your uncles tipped their caps
to themselves in mirrors before stepping out
the door into the busy world they

never recognized beyond the threat
of othering. Others from another other whom
they looked away from in order to smile.

ONE MORE

The small talk invariably dies
in the dark silence of the cab ride
as the cabby from whereabouts

unknown sighs and runs his fingers
across the back of his neck
to say without words that one more

red light, that one more shift scuttling
to and fro, that one more month turning
metered miles into rent money

for some shitty box apartment,
that one more year aging hard
in Los Angeles, this basin of wildfire

smoke and drought and cheerful-
little-airbrushed-billboard
songbirds who refuse to grow up,

Lord in Heaven. There is a moment
in life when each of us becomes
painfully aware of how far we have

left to go, and all we can do is sigh
unconsciously and brace ourselves
on the railing at the bottom of a flight

of stairs that leads to a bedroom
into which we can collapse. The sigh
is the most honest expression a body

can offer because it is involuntary.
The body simply becomes a wealth
of ache and the mind agrees. Green light.

Lone kestrel perched on a wire. Child
with curly hair skipping across
San Vincente. Hollywood grows dark

as any other place on this planet
in predictable intervals, and this driver
and I have more in common than

we'll ever know or admit to. So now,
I sing of him before he's forgotten.
Before he's added to the catalogue

of human sorrow I touch and withdraw
from. The sorrow about which I know
almost nothing. The sorrow of days

twisted into the churn of engine fire
with one hand gripped to a wheel
adrift in an ocean of wheels.

The sorrow of taillights
spinning off into space like twin
red stars at the center of a galaxy

that one day will reach a penultimate
moment then sigh and collapse
and give itself over to the waiting dark.

A Flaming Ford, the Speed of Life

Travis screaming out *Prepare ye the way of the Lord*
at jackrabbits skittering beneath our headlights,
the Messiah coming to Kansas in a flat-head Ford...

— *B.H. Fairchild,* 'Rave On'

LUNCH WITH MY SPIRITUAL ADVISOR AT TIFFANY'S DINER

My advisor says we must learn
to do nothing, according to Merton,
to take possession of our being here
where the world hits fever pitches
daily with gas prices plummeting
further into the asthenosphere
over which Oklahoma is shifting
seismically, and the continent
ties its climate change rate to refresh
rates compounded by global
averages calculated by the EPA,
WHO, who knows, but they affect loans
even on hovels in the hills
of Kentucky, hills Merton once
climbed down from to see
what was becoming of cities
mutinied by advert men clad
with bourbon grins or gin martinis
toasting to the latest technology
half-heartedly, while the little doves
tending Easy-Bake ovens
with Mittens the kitten licking
his genitals on the lounger
or the ottoman, which is all
that remains of the empire,
foot stools, I mean what becomes
of us humans if that can happen
to an entire empire, I ask
my spiritual advisor who doesn't
know he's my spiritual advisor but

who is a Princeton Divinity School grad
nonetheless and who gave me Merton's
essays and said we should discuss
God at our next meeting, and yes,
at the center of my being
is nothingness or everythingness
crammed into a spec that fits
upon the head of a nail driven
into a stud and spackled over
with joint compound, sanded,
then primed and painted to match
curtains or throw pillows inspired
by French countryside châteaus
that nobody within two hundred
miles of this diner has encountered
outside of Pottery Barn catalogues
mailed for free or emailed
to dummy address inboxes that
fill and fill and fill and will never
be emptied or closed, and work
is calling so I put up a finger to
indicate one minute to my advisor,
then this poem is calling my wife
a woman who dreams in blue,
wife who says that even sleep
is no escape from a new season
of *The Walking Dead*, starting tonight,
which is Valentine's Day,
day to honor the Roman saint
who Claudius had beaten, stoned,
and decapitated according
to the Christian Broadcast Network
whose website advertises trips
to Israel, the holy land, a place

my wife once traveled to
the day after I proposed, and in
a market in Jerusalem or Tel Aviv,
who can remember such details,
she witnessed a grown man
masturbating in a three-thousand-
year-old stairwell, circumcised
and public in a way I'll never
fully envision or understand,
praising perhaps the God
of sexual frustration, the God
of cheap trinkets for tourists, the God
we can't erase from collective memory
and can't bury or beat or stone
to death with Grecian marble
unearthed and laid with fortified
thin set on my bathroom floor
at ten dollars a square foot, which
was a fucking steal, grouted with
Delorean gray because I loved the name
more than platinum gray—it had
nothing to do with color—and when
I hang up with work I want
my advisor to say that God
is just who we are when we're alone,
and I want him to weep
with me before the check comes
expeditiously, although speed
has less to do with space-time
and more to do with perception,
to be at a fixed vantage and witness
and say with relative certainty
that the object is moving quickly
or is moving with blinding grace

as my advisor leans in and kisses
me on the cheek or draws a cross
on my forehead with his thumb
and tells me that I'm one
of the good ones, the blessèd
few with the ear of the godhead,
and that whatever crosses my lips
is holy, crosses my mind is holy,
crosses the infernal white of
this page is holy, and that if
I quiet myself long enough, that if
I look hard enough I'll see,
as I'd always suspected,
the gate of heaven is everywhere.

HORSEPOWER RANCH, FOR SALE

Just because we can see the gate doesn't
mean we were meant to enter, but I've got
Google and bandwidth and a set of eyes
that can see what fifteen million dollars buys
is a spread of land in Miller County, Missouri
that spiders off into manicured hills, waterfalls,
and a private runway—caretaker included,
horse stalls posh enough to let four horse
masseuses fit comfortably after the day's
polo match concludes. Everything wood hewn
from walnut harvested onsite assures me
the answer is *no*, we don't belong in these
thoughts where a single head of cattle raises
his head to look at our Toyota with heavy
eyes—he knows full well we're lost and out
of our element or minds to think otherwise.
He chews that sideways chew and lets us scoot
past his little oasis of gravity fed luxury
meant only to feed the class of humans
who can bother Sotheby's for a tour and send
a summa cum laude assistant to white glove
the place and walk the master suite from corner
to corner. You can't think of this ranch as home
when your family is nuclear and simple like mine
and sups delivered pizza and pays bills with grace
periods and is counted among the lucky lot.
Look around and tell me this isn't the ranch
where people like our kind aren't trophy hunted
on corporate getaways—I'm talking Bilderberg
people plotting out centuries of humanity
with secret handshakes and knowing nods—

but if I were being honest I'd say this land is a bit
overvalued, that the soil here is too rocky
to grow more than steaks and Kentucky Derby
equine and I'd prefer to keep mine driving home
to a city named after the patron saint of art,
to a city so strangled it weeps bullets and pills
and strip clubs when the veil of night drops,
and all this American noise keeps spinning
along the radio dial until all I want is static. You
can have all this catered wealth flanked
by dilapidated mid-century RVs eaten
by rattlesnakes and witch grass. All this karstness
dribbling underfoot like a foundation giving
up its supports. All this business of misplaced value
beebopping like one of those inflatable gorillas
lording over used car lots of the disenfranchised
I pass by and judge like cancer judging
a prostate. You can have the lot. I'll keep the beauty
I've already got. You make my leaving easy.

AIR SHOW

Just like any other car in the Home Depot lot,
this lime green Lamborghini Aventador finds

a spot under a porcelain striped, sky-blue sky
on a 60 degree day in May in a valley

that sank under the Mississippi in '93
only to rise again into this outlet-mall

renaissance where we have all come
with coolers and lawn chairs and children,

here to this valley where I once held my nose
until the water slowed back into its banks.

But now *is* today, and a trickster bi-plane rallies
smoke trails until it seems all I've forgotten

has been forgiven. My children ogle warplanes.
My children lack context. Their bewildered

eyes glance upwards at the alien mothership
known as the B-2 Stealth Bomber the same way

the cavalry of World War I looked up
at the whole sky atwitter with dogfights as the ground

shifted beneath hooves. Here lies a floodplain
that no longer floods. There whomps

a Chinook with two sets of blades,
and a Harrier Jump Jet pogos up and down

the runway like a circus elephant with wings
of steel, the whole show playing out like lost

b-roll footage from *Top Gun*, a film that was
nothing more than Tom Cruise's career

sliding one arm into an absurd leather jacket.
Patton, Napoleon, Alexander the Great,

even Achilles himself. When cast under
the dimmest light, don't they all just shrink back

into a failed treatise on free will? How is any age
greater than the hero it forges from iron

then scratches down into song or celluloid, and how
can our existence be proof of anything more

than the success of military parades of the past—a past
where parade goers squealed through flesh and

bone at the uniformed ranks trudging epaulettes
and tanks through commercial districts?

My children are squealing as loud as any.
My children are the relevance we bequeath.

My children are basking like lizards
under the swirl of turbine-induced jetwash,

and tonight they will fall asleep hard—I mean
they will pass the fuck out—sunburned, ears

still ringing—and when I click off the lamps and kiss
each forehead, I'll smell the jet fuel in their hair.

EM DASH

Daydream Johnny's switchblade starting shit,
        the Aaron Burr of punctuation—you enter

every scene like Penelope's snubnosed suitors
        with throats slit and bleeding out into ending,

into interruption, parenthetical and beginning
        like an attention deficit problem-child, like ice

on hot coals raining back down as hailstones
        inside each thunderclap, monstrous storm,

leviathan of the underground tunnels, concrete
        storm sewer bursting forth an unswimmable

current against the boulder smooth creek bed:
        the crawfish antennae, the fisherman's cast

from the lonely pier and of course the pier itself
        thrusting another argument into the Pacific.

Billy club, butcher knife, lead pipe, lipstick, flatline.
        Wild Thing strutting out from centerfield and the high

hard one breaking the strike zone's flimsy walls.
        Riptide, roller coaster jumping the tracks, mainline

delivery of juice and the lineman swaying down
        from a helicopter tether to a tripped transformer

with a song in his electric heart, grounded with rubber.
        You're singing Alpha's answer to Omega, Zeus's

lightning bolt to Hera's hand going up his tunic,
       and you're the steady playing drunk with a pool

cue in the pool hall cracking white cue balls open
       into rainbows. Cigarette on the doorman's lip,

unlit then lit. Movement without just cause,
       skipped heartbeat in the syntax. There's nothing

holding you back from the edge of the cliff
       from which you leap like dynamite and dive.

ABSCONDING TO THE SANCTUARY IN PENNSYLVANIA WITH THE OPTIMISM OF RICK STEVES

It's worth investing in a decent pair of boots before
you try escaping through space and time to stop for once
and greet again the politics of the water cycle. I'm talking
about alighting your pocket with a journal and pencil
and wearing the countenance of a disciple of Walden
by burying yourself in bird song and bear scrapings. I'm
talking about rainbowing in the morning by Niagara's
many falls before pushing highway cruise through
and beyond the bustle of cities until you voila upon
a dirt road dipping its swerve into juniper dapple falling
upon shingles laden with mosses and fairy sprout
mushrooms that beard this historic Watres Lodge.
I'm talking about the footpath uphill from Lacawac
Lake's pristine, flat and rowable face far from
the choked stacks and forever post-industrial ennui
of Scranton PA. I'm talking about ditching
the family as they drift perchance into afternoon
nap to trundle down to the dock under the halo
of a black umbrella, and with each nettled step forward
over rivulets running to meet the carved out body
of lake, you must work to change yourself to the liking
of the place. You must leave behind hand wringing
and derivative actions and create ripples from your
center like the dimpling of raindrops upon a lake
that you're finally able to see: clear to the bottom
in most places so the fish can look up at your wavy
form as though you were an old friend come to visit.
Look at you up there! You look like the washed out
ghost of youth gone by. Like an opaque window

separating the factory floor from sky. You better grab
an oar in each hand and remember that a splinter
in your thumb is a muse worth asking to dance, and
before your family wakes or the phone in your pocket
calls you back to some ordained task of scatological
import—be militant now, let the rain soak through
your clothes as you create those little succulent
eddies with each stroke against the fulcrum of oarlocks
and get as far away from the shore as you can
before making the honest mistake of looking back.

HOW TO MAKE ACORN FLOUR

— for Rob Connoley

Sure, it's not news that the presidential
candidates speak in loose platitudes,
but if you can add two tablespoons
of acorn flour to your biscuits?
Well, now you've got something.
Hear that thunking on your roof?
Listen, and sure enough you'll hear it.
It's acorn season friend, which
may or may not be true, but
if it is, get out there and beat back
the squirrels and take your share.
Besides, those rodents are a bunch
of freeloaders who'd sooner gnaw
a hole into your attic for the winter
than share their stockpile—so if they
yell at you? You, yell back. Fill a bucket,
whatever size you got. Shell them nuts
and go ahead and nibble the meat.
Terrible, right? You'll need to leach
the terrible out of those young nuts—
pretend it's like seventh grade geometry
class all over again, but don't pretend
a right angle means there's a square.
You failed geometry and you're failing
at immortality in your own time, bits of you
sifted to the bottom of an egg timer. But
as far as the acorns, leach them good.
Like a week at least, changing the water
daily and tucking them deep in the fridge.
After the week has come and gone,

blend and sieve them through cheesecloth.
And you thought you were too busy?
Too important maybe, or like, who needs
a trade when you have Amazon Prime?
But look at you standing in the kitchen with
a towel looped lazily over one shoulder.
You're emptying the blended meat
onto a baking sheet and baking on low
for four hours. I once read a Kooser poem
about how to make rhubarb wine, and
he suggested having a beer while you wait,
but that was just him filling a line. Make
sure you sift the clumps when it's done
but that's pretty much it, and now you've
got flour from acorns. Face it, you been
crunching over these things your whole
life thinking about the mightiness
of the human foot and the splintering
helplessness of those little shells,
but what a delight to dip the nose
of a measuring spoon into the flour
to add the last ingredient to a recipe
for something you just invented.

ELEGY FOR ALICE WHILE HOOKING A PRIMITIVE RUG

Whatever pattern you're hoping to create, it's best
       to hook your background last, so as not to distract
from your focal point, which in this case is Alice

       propped up at a window like an alabaster statuette
on Waterman Ave. listening for the sound of lions
       scoring noon at the St. Louis Zoo. It's important

to keep hooking just inside your pattern's outline,
       otherwise it will grow too large too quickly, like
an 18-year-old in a wedding gown, courtship

       an inline-four-cylinder engine between her legs,
five children clambering to fill a house.
       There are constellations named after lesser

saints, and those stars only come out at night
       when it's clear, when the family has taken the boat
out on the Mississippi, docking and camping under

       a canopy of army-green canvas. Soon you'll have
the shape of an elderly woman. Design, hook, and bind her.
       When she comes into focus, loop after loop,

remember that she was young once, too, knew what it meant
       to compromise completely. When you've finished,
steam the piece you've made, whipstitch the edges,

       and sew it flush. Hang it somewhere it will be seen.

MECHANICAL ISSUE

— at O'Hare International Airport

A connection nozzle retracts improperly, and thusly,
we stranded passengers idle, plug in our devices to keep

them alive and tingling, and our heads rise in unison
at each microphone crackle from the gate like a street

of umbrellas opening simultaneously. Predawn winces
into daylight, shiftworkers rotate into twilight, the moon

becomes a pimentoed olive hovering above a dirty
gin martini. Our tribe gives up, disbands. The muzak

escalates to a purgatorial soundtrack composed for
weary deadheads left like wild apples to rot,

and we hold our hands out to receive complimentary
veggie wraps rationed in the old soup-line style

as luggage bearers march past towards unbroken planes,
and the gods of takeoff aim each jet skyward like

javelin throwers practicing drunk and naked at midnight.
The television near our gate shows us we're not alone.

CNN explains why the Statue of Liberty went dark,
but everyone has seen shoddy work, knows faulty

wiring disrupts the circuit, and the fountain water
here tastes like water endemic to the delivery system.

We look to the television for answers, but the statue
stays dark and darker madnesses begin to swirl.

Some hayseed from Kentucky curses under his breath
in a wild language native to himself, and we who're left

get sorted into a standby line believing our homes
are not hopes nor things with feathers, but simply the heels

of our shoes clicking three times together in desperation.
This day will end, but it's unpredictable how or where.

BUZZFEED

Took three hours to scroll a page on Buzzfeed
all the way down to the bottom rung
of internets where boarding school
adverts for Exeter and Shattuck were hiding out
like the bad Jacks in a back alley that send kids
knuckles up to Brown and Harvard
to learn what billionaires give away isn't
much they don't plan on taking back anyway
in the high-noon-daily-free-for-all-blood-thirst-
first-person-Wall-Street shootemup: hustlers,
they're going to hustle, cause we all know deft
little marble busts built to adorn sarcophagi
aren't cheap, and neither are graves with custom
solar-powered alarm systems forever free
from the grid of grave-robbing dignitaries,
such as yours truly. The glory divine goes
to the kings and lords. All hail the bedwetters
who tie bowtie knots right out the gates
and don't scroll down where I found internets
hiding mischief so digital and corporal
that mine eyes became thine shepherd in the syntax
screaming *ACTIVE SHOOTER*, active
shooter who then takes a bow and
flips the switch to inactive suddenly,
who drips like honeydew into Whole Foods
for a quick lunch and job application,
where he or she or you or we might crush
learning curves for the home-baked unionizers,
clerks, stackers, baggers and trolley fetchers
who usher in the new era of the vegan beast
and watch Day-Glo-boomer-born aisle browsers

who keep licking rib thin the last bits
of baby fat from babies. Five minutes from the sandy
bottom, scrolling down to the Buzzfeed of internets,
I reached out both arms like a ninja
warrior climbing Mount Midoriyama sours
cut with a tonic spritz at the Luxor afterparty
confab of pre-forgotten celebrity, where all
was still impossible and the bottom was rising
up at me like a trick floor and the walls
coming in like that Star Wars trash compactor
pressing me into the shape of shapes
that only took thirty days on a treadmill
with luxury-condo timeshares in Tahiti
baiting me, and me skeezing over to the Gymboree
and churning out one thousand impromptu
cartwheels. Not Bieber. Not Biggie. Not Bilbo.
Not the drug of the century sent to cleanse
the war on sobriety with one swift
sniff up the schnozzola. Not the car-wash
blowjob lasting three minutes of rainbow
sudded windshield harmonics. Not
the universe bellied up to the state bar
exam and failing to miss even
so much as a beat on the eighty-five-hour
commute—as in, how long is too long?
Not the rich nor the poor nor the boneheaded
middle class who always forgets to renew
their memberships to public radio in the classist
dick move of being 'too busy'—you had one
stinking job to do, one lousy stinking life to live,
one ruse to bruise the peach come summer,
and there I whistle by in my top hat scrolling midnight
right on through the other side like I'm playing
Punch-A-Bunch on *Price is Right*, the Bob Barker

days, that thin-phallused microphone
and the sequined assistants we all knew should've
filed #metoo lawsuits against his ass like three
seasons ago. But down I went until Buzzfeed
gave up and became Buzzsaw the Jackstraw,
the second coming of Yahoo, and we all knew
daylight would come before I reached
the end of that scroll, knew the only trick old Satan
ever played was convincing us the computer
before us existed and wasn't just another
emoji-faced polliwog, just another racecar Jesus,
just another shaggy shaggy throw rug under our feet
with those long little fibers curling up like soft grass
between the toes, so real we felt
like somehow we were actually touching solid ground.

The Checkered Flag Comes Quickly

Only where the religion goes on without a god
And the sandwich is wolfed down without a blessing,
I think of us bowing at the table there:
The grand patriarch of the family holding forth
In staunch prayer, and the potato pie I worshipped.
The sweeter the pie, the shorter the prayer.

— *Rodney Jones, 'The Kitchen Gods'*

DINNER WITH MY SPIRITUAL
ADVISOR AT PEACEMAKER

Landlocked lobster shack we can't afford
but turn up to anyway and order the clam
chowder and try to describe what dying
as gesture means: symbolism, objectified
and affixed to the crucifix resting atop
the bosom of Karla, monastic nun
turned spitfire cabaret dancer three
nights a week at the Atomic Cowboy.
I watched her ruffle and kick once and
my head sang like a calliope, I say between
spoonfuls of chowder, and he says, Jesus
wasn't just some pushover—he doesn't say
radical, but I love visualizing the fringe hero
of humanity locked on a crash course
with the tip of a Roman spear. A couple
wearing lobster-boil bibs around their necks
look happier than two stones skipping
upon the surface of a calm lake as they suck
buttered bits of claw meat down their gullets,
bits broken microscopic and spirited
through blood vessels that if, laid end on end,
could map out an ancient trade route
stretching twice around the globe.
I imagine camps of travelers with camels
warming themselves by fires together
and telling stories of Jesus the outsider,
Lord of the axe grinder, God turned man
turned shit disturber ready to upend
Heaven and Earth for the sake
of humankind. I love the quiet bravado

of saviors who die before we can know them.
I look at the walls around me and see only
whitewashed bricks and think maybe
the bricks listen. I point to the wall and say,
maybe each brick is like another ear
of God tuned to the conversations of man.
Or maybe they dream of the wrecking ball,
he says, which tells me that he's given up
on the delusion of control, that he's finally
rolled back the stone and is waiting
for his turn to rise. Through the canyon
of buildings I hear the echo of an engine
throttling into high gear above the churn
of highway noise and feel my own blood
careening closer to my heart like an F1 racer
hitting a sudden rise in the track too fast,
all four tires going airborne at once.
Sometimes I've hurt myself on purpose.
Sometimes I think we're driven toward
doom by virtue of the Earth beneath
us with all our bodies and histories twirling
on its fingertips like an amateur plate spinner
and speeding along a cosmic route through
an expanding or contracting universe
that passes before us like the blinking eyes
of an audience at an annual conference
of quantum physicists who are waiting
for the keynote speaker to stop blathering
and take a drink of water. What is nobility
but the reward for patience?
What is consciousness but the cooled ash
after the fire aware of how it got there?
I'm tired of burning. I'm tired of being cooled.
I want to give my advisor the answers

he's looking for but I am a ruin of questions.
Where once there was a temple, only pillars.
Where once a roof, now only clouds
and darkness interrupted by the jest of stars.

THE EMPTY CUBE

Imagine a cube with glass on all sides
and nothing but air between.
Is there room inside where one can hide

the way a mouth that slowly opens wide
can also reveal a scream?
Imagine a room with glass on all sides

where patience and stillness collide
with the absence of scene
leaving space inside where one can hide.

To fall in love with virtue is pride.
To falter is to fuck things up again.
Imagine a space with glass on all sides,

a walled off cube wherein a man resides.
He was late today for work again.
He has almost nowhere left to hide.

To obey is a sign he's already died.
Defiance is far more interesting.
Even in a room with glass on all sides
there's always somewhere left to hide.

LATE FOR WORK

Ten minutes, sure, nobody notices a thing,
but when hours stack up your work
gets conveyored off to the next in line,

and soon your absences begin flickering
across reports like June bugs gone belly up,
which causes a stir among managers who huddle

around a conference table like primary
and secondary colors on a wheel.
After a week, your workload redistributes

itself entirely, which is the natural inclination
for work. You obviously didn't expect
the world to wait around, but they're curious.

Maybe you've escaped to a wooded glen,
or slumped yourself over a second-rate craps table
in Tahoe like a scene ripped from an unrealized

Hopper painting. Maybe you just plucked
a crow's feather and boarded a plane for Tibet. Point is,
it's anybody guess, and what matters most is that you

are not here, and here there is a framed photo
of guinea pigs next to the monitor where you
are being erased from the system

by a man following protocol in human resources
named Bill Weathers. His guinea pigs
are dressed up like Samson and Delilah

for a Halloween picture because he loves them,
so what? Tell me what you've loved deeply
enough to give an existence, to that is as profound

as those two costumed rodents? There's more
to life than the one you've been given,
and you've fallen out of that one almost

completely. Decades ago you kissed someone
profoundly goodbye forever and didn't
care who saw you bawl like a love-sick idiot

as you ran back to your car in the parking lot.
The children you may have had together.
The sad trope of growing out of your twenties.

The house you could have built or rehabbed
to your liking. All of those boring, provincial,
middle-aged trappings no longer threatened

you here—here where you no longer are.
The place you used to show up to on time.
The place you even once professed to love.

HAMMOCK WITH THREE-EIGHTHS INCH GALVANIZED CHAIN

The store's got this metal beaked machine
for snipping off lengths from heavy reels of chain
that's supposed to be operated by *employees
only*, but I've already got my length drawn out
and I'm terrible about following rules and also
it doesn't take a genius I think to operate its
pneumatic pressure without cutting one's finger
completely off with the business end, although,
truth be told, I'm a bit distracted and prone
to inner flights of mania. For example,
the light here, which comes from all angles
and seems to obliterate shape and form and color.
Also, I'm sober for once and trying to stay out
of my own way and be a reliable, middle-aged
version of myself—hence the hammock
I bought and aim to string up between trees
and lounge upon in the fading evening. Hence
the chain and the beak that snips the links
at seven feet with unexpected ease—I catch
the broken links, tuck them in my pocket,
and wind up the chain and am suddenly thinking
about the monks I used to see grocery shopping
in the mountains of California, and how I used
to imagine them putting on robes in the mornings
and fixing tight a pair of sandal straps
to go out and kiss the stone toes of Buddha
in the monastery garden. They smooth over time,
don't they? The toes under those prayerful lips?
Facing each day and conceiving patience from light?
And now, as I'm waiting in line to checkout,

I can't help but imagine they too would appreciate
the soft fabric of a hammock holding their body aloft
and the lengths of galvanized chain and forgiving trees.
Each part of it necessary and never far from mind.

LETTER TO THE NOBEL COMMITTEE FOR LITERATURE AT THE SWEDISH ACADEMY

I don't need your praise to survive, but
disappear with me south down Highway 63
from Rolla to Tecumseh until the trees
swirl phantasmagoric and you'll see
the ground open up to a merry-go-round
of rural depletion, isolation and poverty,
(not isolated to this part of the country),
and greenest yet are the teeth of glass
blinking hollow in the filling stations, alas
of yesteryear, lazy screen doors flapping
against the burnt shells of methlabian
double-wides. Choose to come or don't,
but a cozier more spurious glen won't
be unearthed in the lines of Eliot's
The Waste Land still writhing in waste bins
of juggernaut Wal-Marts and Rural Kings
that don't mean a thing to steal from.
Imagine how it feels to come of age
in the fallout of Egyptian royalty, eyes
looking out from the floating capstones
of pyramids on the lowest denomination
of currency. Imagine all these full-throttled
engines of consumerism and greed
left pistonless in the dusty confines of
Missouri, which is my constant state
of being, and in case you were wondering,
the otherwise docile trout fishing rivers
still rise and rise above the ancient empty
streets far too potholed for dreamers or

farmers or high-school cattle queens
riding makeshift parade floats into front-
page, fish-wrapper oblivion. Nobody wants
to sound ungrateful. Kids here just wanna
play pickup sticks and jacks until puberty
paints a few patches of fur to their genitals
and then age into belief structures set up
before them like mansions for superchurch
pastors pounding out hymns and lurching
back into private-jet business wire transfers
to Zurich, city which sounds like a made-up word
for the yet undiscovered moon orbiting
Jupiter to human minds that can only suffer
so much knowledge before giving up
and trying to bluff their losing hands. The Bible
in every Motel 6 could catch fire and burn
this country to the ground, or this letter
could unhinge the heavy doors locking
away the cosmic energy, could spin you
like a top for hours or simply turn you north,
away from the sweetwater abyssal urinal
cakes of truck stops glittering with the digital
magnetism of Youtube ivy-league lectures
on macroeconomic trend-line averages
in commodities markets too hot to touch
without capital-growth indices buffering
the retirement packages of the middle
class, cattle class, cud-chewing class, four
stomachs wide and filled with ammonia-
soaked beef-like patties, could swing through
the fields into dominoed picturesque suburban
dalliance and table-sized pizzas for gridiron
couch surfing Sundays. Not rich, just fat
in an otherwise obese world. Not blousy,

just closeted in a loose weave of giggle fiber
piped in from the Silicon Valleys of the future.
We don't wonder where you are anymore, and
even if you decide to come, it's only a moment,
and soon enough your committee will figure out
how to escape and head north to the taiga forests
grown microwavable, in the tropical sense
of the word, but out of this country entirely
into the shipyards of Nova Scotia where
you can build from hand-hewn lumber a boat
to journey back across the North Atlantic
into waiting walled-in rooms so decadently
adorned you'll probably forget you'd ever left
at all, which is where I'm going to leave you,
because this is not a story to pass on and I've
got a lot of other stuff to do. Please, don't get up,
                           I'm only passing through.

STORM SEWER

A sewer system designed by engineers
funnels rain to this low point in the valley,
channels storms through a dragon's throat
until what roars forth is both the fury
and wrath of the Old Testament God.
On the concrete ledge above the froth
of thrashing spit stands a boy who knows
that death is only a toe slip away, that if he
touches the creek he will understand death
but that death, too, will understand him.
The boy never looks away, never moves,
stands forever on the edge of this moment
measuring himself against the strength of water.

THE READING

— at the University of Missouri Columbia, 2005

When Philip Levine scooted up to the lectern
sporting a pair of nurse's shoes (comfy, white,
slip-resistant), I have to admit I was worried.
Cause you see, I'd driven through the spleen

of Missouri to watch heaven unshackle
his mortal tongue for half an hour or so,
and so those shoes and that old-man scoot
made me worry that I'd come too late.

It's worth mentioning that almost nobody
likes poems about the poor, literature
of displacement, and also there's little
interest in working-poor poems either,

but the poor still exist and so did Levine
whose tongue began moving inside his
closed mouth as he kind of ferryboated
up to that hunk of mahogany. Christ!

Where did he think he'd landed? Hand
decorated bronze sconces affixed
to floor-length oak-paneled walls,
the Midwest trying to con itself again?

It's worth mentioning that almost nobody
cares for poems about the Midwest
either. Imagine people saying *flyover
country* and flittering their little eyes

like they'd seen a taxidermied animal
mounted above the bar at Mississippi Flyway.
Coincidentally, they're often the same
people who've never stubbed a toe

drunkenly on a thing and kicked the thing
with the same toe they'd just stubbed.
But that's an academic argument.
At the time, I didn't know anything

about the academy and was painting
bedrooms of mansions for a living so I
knew the cost of things. Levine set down
his book and coughed like a front loader

dumping river stone into a truck bed,
and yeah, I'd read his bio. I knew he'd
been holed up in middle-of-nowhere
Fresno teaching all the future Daphne's

and Ogden's of America to break
lines for the lion's share of his life,
and that each poem where he imagined
himself twenty years old again was like

my dad retelling me stories about
the summers he worked the line at Chrysler
to pay his way through college, the very
college to which I'd come to see Levine speak.

It's worth mentioning the privilege
of my own reflection here does not
escape me. That this poem is not for
people who don't read poems but

for those who do, and that when Levine
finally spoke and tried to define *work*
for the room he was actually extolling
the price everyone pays to wake up each day

and talking about love and the capacity
for true human connection to people
who nodded knowingly and applauded
at the end of the reading only, which

is customary, like a carving knife placed
at the head of the table, a nicety proffered
to the one with the words on the open page,
the quiet signature of the educated class.

FRAMEWORK

We'd found ourselves in Memphis, Cologne,
Boston, then Lyon. We discovered churches,
escarpments, hillsides burnt to stubble and
the ruins of local bars flattened to rubble
for the onset of strip malls and boutique hotels.
We watched as trauma entered like detox
sweats on the third night, how it twisted
into a metaphor for the orchards and vineyards
and barnyards left to rot thanks to the usual
vehicles of displacement that rolled in from
out of state with bags of cash and bad plates.
We scratched like hens for love. We wasted
our time and money in the supermarkets.
We convinced ourselves that we knew
the firmament from the face of the lake
because that was a lie we could live with.

But suddenly, the tone was all wrong. We
were mid-life roustabouts debuting in white
at the dilettante ball. The salesman was our
father knocking on suburban doors with
tight knuckles and wrecking balls for fists.
We looked around in terror and saw the walls
were white as the emptiness surrounding
a stanza, and then we collectively blinked.
What changed in us was more feeling
than fact, more fog than mist. We lit a candle
in the basilica and flipped our collar up
as we pushed open the heavy wooden doors
stepping out into a street full of pedestrians
and shop windows refracting sunlight. It was

morning again, and each step forward
brought the world that much more into focus.

PLANNED OBSOLESCENCE

noun: a policy of producing consumer goods that rapidly become
obsolete and so require replacing, achieved by frequent changes
in design, termination of the supply of spare parts, and the use of
nondurable materials.

— from Oxford Languages by way of Google

Mont Blanc or Monte Bianco
remains the highest mountain
in the Alps for now, but for how long?
It's not a dishwasher because
it's a mountain, just being a mountain,
but perhaps from the right angle of light
in winter it can be a new style of hat
the Earth has put on for a formal outing.
Say the universe was collapsing, which
it might very well be, what kind of formal
coming-of-age celebration might bring
with it the need for a ballroom? Waltz
or foxtrot? Roses or lilacs? Bowtie
or cravat? Our planet donning its
ordinary mountain, the heavens
in a sparkling Paris plunge: how long
can they keep from making eye contact?

Are you still there? I'm asking you
point blank in the middle of a poem
if you can help me identify where
the failure has occurred and whether
you'd like to spend the weekend trying
to fix it or are you more inclined
to run to the store and replace the thing
altogether? Look at us. Aren't we quite

the pair. Lately I've noticed a decline
in the centipede population around
our house and Regina said that's just
in the basement and I said I've always
imagined the basement population
of insects as kind of a spillover
representation of the outdoor
population but I also have no idea
what I'm doing. I mean, I have no basis
in reality for the statement other
than tacit observation and half-formed
theorizing of the domestic variety.

Have you ever gone walnut bowling?
Of course you haven't. But around here
we've nicknamed a nearby street
Walnut Lane in spite of the fact that
it's already been named after the French
general Lafayette, not that he ever
walked there, which is weird, right?
Naming things after people who've
never had any formal business dealings
with the things named after them?
But there's a big walnut tree and each
season it drops its bounty and we
scoop them up and roll them suckers
across Brentwood Boulevard—some
don't make it across, some do.

My kids are learning a thing or two
about Greek myth the old-fashioned way.
I become Hephaestus slagging away
on some iron and Cora slips in like
she's got some business with me but she's

just old crafty Prometheus, you know.
Then James swoops in playing Zeus
with a bag full of leg irons and a bird
on his shoulder looking like some kind
of god that pirates might pray to.
The story is the one you know. The kids
are simply playing their roles and me?
Well, I'm here stealing a bit of that lesson
to show you what it's like to make
believe when you've morphed into
a full-grown adult with the early
nibblings of arthritis in your hands.

Where did that mountain go? The one
from earlier in the poem? Can a person
loiter somewhere they've been invited?
Do people still plant gardens according
to the lunar cycle or has that method
been scrapped altogether? Will the rains
continue where you live when the water
wars come to fruition or do you envision
a more nomadic existence? It's anyone's
guess how the next few decades
are going to play out. Most models
aren't particularly rosy, but a person can't
put their underwear on in a model. Imagine
the person's just showered and dried off.
They're standing sideways in the mirror
looking at themselves naked and heavier
in the dimmed wattage of morning.
They sigh. They suck in. They relax.

WINE FRIDGE

A wine fridge, used gently, free for pickup
on Craigslist; it rests there because, quite simply,
capitalism requires that such novelties accrue
when the middle class suffers a glut of bonus
income come February, and I don't know how
much cheap wine fits inside, but Kendall Jackson
comes to mind as the only bulk white I recall
from the country club where I worked banquets
at sixteen so I could afford to #heymister beer
and gun it across the county line and disappear,
for what it was worth, into a bonfire where
I must've said at least a dozen times, *Fuck*
this penguin outfit or *Fuck those goddamned*
rich-ass motherfuckers or *Pass me a smoke,*
I got a light. Still, that wine fridge will never
cross my lawn, let alone front-door threshold,
the same way my sixteen-year-old self will
never give up chain smoking or believing
in the beautiful death or staring bewilderedly
out from inside my body's bones at what's left
of him that I've kept shelved in a plastic bin
on the unfinished side of the basement. A few
pictures and a journal. Maybe a soccer trophy?
His disappointment will just have to get in line
with the rest of me, because old age crushes
boutonnières into the shape of a wine fridge,
a fucking fridge designed for the purpose
of keeping wine at less than room temperature.
I hate wine. And yet here it is now, smack dab
in the middle of my poem, which is just what
I need. One more absurd, impossible thing
I have somehow been charged with getting rid of.

O PIE DIVINE

All bakers should be taught to sing.
— Robert Hass, from a poem remembering what Tomaž Šalamun
once said

Work drunk or exhausted, nobody
could tell, but fresh off an all-night shift
on Christmas Eve this old baker burst
from the back doors of the bakery belting
out his own version of *O Holy Night*
to the line of us waiting along Edwards Street.

Under the light of a lamppost, he sang *pie*
in place of *night* like some street-corner
Pavarotti to a line in which I waited
for my three loaves of Shampa
and half-dozen cannolis, and he just
kept on singing of *crusts softly browning*.

This man, perfumed with bread yeast, who
seemed to be dragging a raft of years
behind him in the right knee he favored,
could have simply disappeared to any one
of the shotgun houses around the corner
and fried up sausage links, a few eggs

with lace, in peace, before retiring
to the mattress that held the shape
of a human form for him to fall
back into, back into the light of morning.
But instead, he stood and sang proudly,
and the continents shook loose

underfoot as we stood in the throng
with our individual thermoses of coffee
and petty family grievances ready
to rise again inside each kitchen,
icicle lights dangling outside living
room windows, windows frosted to glisten,

but then we heard this baker reach
the high crescendo of *O Pie Divine*,
followed by a quick bow and quicker exit
that felt like the moon ducking behind
a bank of clouds. This man who up
and vanished like some working-class god

who'd only come down from the heavens
to lay his little tune like an offering
at our feet upon an ordinary sidewalk,
song for the ears of us foolish mortals
who assumed, as usual, we were waiting there
that morning for something else altogether.

THE LICE

And behold the lice set upon our house
like the fire of a thousand suns burning,
because an imaginary itch can turn real
if you imagine hard enough. Have you ever
seen the wallpaper crawl? Felt the mind
wrinkle and shrink as it tries to comprehend
imagined or imaginary crawly nothings
whistling up the railroad tracks of your spine
like freeloaders bound for the year of plenty
in the wild scalp? Have you ever cinched
the zip ties to the lips of 50-gallon trash bags
stuffed with stuffed animals or parted the hair
of children with steel combs for what red fleck,
what red bounce might feed within dander
locks—because everything has a source,
because everything living feeds from the body
of many, from the blood of the child who visited
our house and wore the wig, the tiara, and
the plastic gunny sergeant's helmet with
Born to Kill written on the back. I'm not
a genius, but I've learned this one lesson
from the Bible: there's more than one way
to kill anything. How the Lord Almighty
could just gameday audible between fire
and plague and on a whim change his mind
and lay down a flood to whip the evil loose from
the bushes. I've learned, too, that a child is just
a child, but the one who showed up to our house
for the birthday cake hurrah carrying lice
in a ponytail was so much more. Hyperbole
to call her a curse upon our house, but a curse

upon our house just the same. So we set off
like a family possessed after getting the call
from the child's mother offering apology for lice,
set off for the whatnots, the parting gifts,
the one to grow on that her child may or may
not have left behind in our house, and today
I'm proud to say our house is clean. Listen,
I don't need to tell you that a thing cannot live
forever. If you're old enough to read this,
you're old enough to know that you simply
choke a thing off at the source, and it will die.
No matter how small. No matter how sublime.

NOTES

'Breakfast with My Spiritual Advisor at Sunny Side Café' quotes both William Shakespeare and William Blake respectively.

'Lunch with My Spiritual Advisor at Tiffany's Diner' borrows some moments from Thomas Merton's 'Conjectures of a Guilty Bystander' and also adapts a line from C.K. Williams' poem 'Spit' that goes, 'God is what it is when we're alone.'

'Horsepower Ranch, For Sale' owes some debt to both Philip Levine's poem 'You Can Have It' and Campbell McGrath's book *American Noise*.

'How to Make Acorn Flower' references a Ted Kooser poem 'How to Make Rhubarb Wine' that also served as inspiration.

'Letter to the Nobel Committee for Literature at the Swedish Academy' borrows some lines and moments from Bob Dylan, Toni Morrison, and Louise Glück.

'O Pie Divine' references Missouri Bakery, which was founded by the Gambaro brothers and has served the Italian American immigrant enclave in St. Louis known as The Hill since 1923. The epigraph from the poem is from the poem 'Poem Not an Elegy in a Season of Elegies' by Robert Hass.

Dedications: The three spiritual advisor poems are dedicated to Chris Nation; 'Air Show' is dedicated to Tom Cruise; 'Elegy for Alice While Hooking a Primitive Rug' is dedicated to the memory of Alice Webb; 'The Reading' is dedicated to the memory of Philip Levine; 'Planned Obsolescence' is dedicated to my children, Cora Mossotti and James Mossotti; 'Wine Fridge' is dedicated to the memory of Eavan Boland; 'O Pie Divine' is dedicated to the memory of my grandmother Elizabeth Mossotti.

ACKNOWLEDGMENTS

A special thanks to the following publications where some of these poems appeared (some in slightly different versions):

Agenda: 'One Art' & 'Horsepower Ranch, For Sale'
basalt: 'Absconding to the Sanctuary in Pennsylvania with the Optimism of Rick Steves'
Bennington Review: 'Dinner with My Spiritual Advisor at Peacemaker' & 'The Empty Cube'
diode: 'Your Racist Uncles' & 'Planned Obsolescence'
Epoch: 'Elegy for Alice While Hooking a Primitive Rug'
Florida Review (Aquifer): 'Breakfast with My Spiritual Advisor at Sunny Side Café' & 'Art Fair'
Iron Horse Literary Review: 'Air Show'
Italian Americana: 'The Lice'
Moon City Review: 'Framework'
Poetry Ireland Review: 'Wine Fridge'
Southeast Review: 'Superior Oak Ridge Landfill'
Southern Review: 'Black Horse, White Horse, Both Plastic'

'Wine Fridge' appeared in *Narcissus Americana* and is reprinted here with permission from the University of Arkansas Press. 'Absconding to the Sanctuary in Pennsylvania with the Optimism of Rick Steves' was written during an artist residency at Lacawac Sanctuary Field Station and Environmental Education Center in Pennsylvania.

Poems in this book have benefited from the support of fellowships, grants, and residencies from the Regional Arts Commission, the Sustainable Arts Foundation, the Artist Residency at Lacawac Sanctuary, the Living Earth Collaborative at Washington University.

There are literally hundreds of people who've touched my life and made it worthwhile. People who shaped me, knowingly or not, and by extension these poems: please know that I love you and am grateful and look forward to seeing you and hearing from you again.

Particular gratitude goes out to: my first readers Kerry James Evans, James Kimbrell, and Regina Mossotti; to Naomi Shihab Nye, Adrian Matejka, James Crews, Erin Quick, Stefene Russell, Katy Balma, and the Tick Tock Poets for their correspondence, guidance and friendship; to my mentors Rodney Jones, David Clewell (in memory), Allison Joseph, Jon Tribble (in memory), and Judy Jordan; to my fellow Salukis Mark Brewin, Hannah New, Amie Whittemore, and so many others; to Jason Eng Hun Lee, Todd Swift, Amira Ghanim, Edwin Smet, and all the good folks at Eyewear and the Black Spring Press Group; to my parents, brothers, sisters, in-laws and extended family who've helped shape me behind the scenes; to my brother Josh for his collaborative workshops and creative symbiosis; to my wife Regina, daughter Cora and son James for their enduring love and patience—you mean everything to me.